Mediterranean Diet for

Vegans

Delicious Soul Satisfying Mediterranean Vegan

Recipes for Weight Loss and a Healthy Lifestyle

Disclaimer

Book description

This book is written with the sole purpose of introducing you to Mediterranean Vegan recipes. If you are a vegan and looking for interesting recipes to add to your daily diet, then this is the perfect book for you! You will be surprised at the wide plethora of choices that are available for vegans that lie within the confines of the Mediterranean diet.

The recipes are all easy to make and will debunk the myth that vegans are pressed for choice when it comes to flavors and seasonings. These recipes have been curated to suit a wide palate. You will have the chance to incorporate the different recipes into your daily meals and won't have to get bored of your diet. You can kiss your monotony goodbye and incorporate meals that will keep your palate happy!

You need not limit yourself to just the recipes mentioned here and can come up with some of your own. As long as you make use of the same ingredient list, you will have a fun time experimenting and creating unique vegan dishes. If you like this book, then you can share it with your friends and family members.

The vegan diet is a very healthy diet to adopt and one that is sure to help you maintain a healthy body. The recipes can also be adopted by people who are not hardcore vegans and so, vegan or not, you are sure to fall in love with this recipe book!

Table of Contents

Disclaimer..3

Book description..5

Table of Contents...7

Introduction...12

Chapter 1: Mediterranean Vegan Pastes, Sauces, and
Dips...15

    Cilantro Pistou 15

    Tahini Paste.. 17

    Tahini Sauce.. 19

    Bell Pepper, Olive, and Arugula Salsa..................... 21

    Hummus.. 23

    Lebanese Moutabel 25

    Cilantro Garlic Hummus............................... 28

    Avocado Taco Dip Recipe 30

Baba Ganoush 32

Lebanese Muhammara 34

Chapter 2: Mediterranean Vegan Breakfast Recipes....37

Focaccia Bread.. 37

Vegan Shakshouka... 41

Mediterranean Breakfast Couscous 45

Cheesy Mediterranean Scramble 47

Zucchini and Mushroom Frittata 49

Mediterranean Quinoa 52

Italian Scramble 54

Cioccolata Calda (Italian Hot Chocolate) 57

Chapter 3: Mediterranean Vegan Salad Recipes.........60

Minty Winter Tabbouleh................................. 60

Greek Salad 62

Big Italian salad 64

Lebanese Fattoush.. 67

Mediterranean Salad 69

Moroccan Carrot and Chickpea Salad 71

Chapter 4: Mediterranean Vegan Soup Recipes.........74

Giouvarlakia (Greek Meatball Soup)...................... 74

Mediterranean Stew 78

Egyptian Red Lentil Soup.. 81

Mediterranean Bean Soup.. 83

Italian Wedding Soup 85

Zuppa Vegana 88

Avgolemano (Greek Easter Soup) 91

Lebanese Lentil Soup... 94

French Onion Soup 97

Moroccan Lentil Soup.. 99

Chapter 4: Mediterranean Vegan Appetizers
Recipes...102

Greek Fava 102

Mediterranean Stuffed Mushrooms 104

Italian Bruschetta with Sautéed Mushrooms 106

Spanish Patatas Bravas 108

Lebanese Shish Taouk (Vegan Shish Kebabs) 110

Chapter 5: Mediterranean Vegan Main Course.........114

Greek Spetsofai.. 114

Mujadara with Lebanese Salata 117

Spanish Paella Primavera.. 120

Cauliflower Shawarma.. 123

Syrian Mehshi Jazzar 127

Egyptian Koshari 131

Lebanese Moussaka 133

Chapter 6: Mediterranean Vegan Dessert Recipes.....135

Mediterranean Halva Pudding 135

Spanish Sangria Dessert.. 138

Italian Castagnaccio (Chestnut Cake).................... 140

French Apple Tart... 143

French Toast Bread Pudding................................... 145

Egyptian Apple Halawa 147

Syrian Baklava 149

Conclusion…………………………………………...153

Introduction

Most people are apprehensive about adopting the vegan diet due to the myths surrounding it. People believe that vegans have to deal with a very restricted ingredient list and make dishes that lack flavor. However, this is just a myth and one that has absolutely no truth to it.

In this book, you will be introduced to a whole world of vegan recipes that will help you beat your monotony. The recipes all lie within the confines of a "Mediterranean Diet". The Mediterranean diet refers to foods that were consumed by the Greeks and Italians in the early 60s. This diet is well known to make people healthy and enhance their longevity.

The vegan diet specializes in incorporating only vegetarian ingredients and leaves out meat and animal-derived products such as milk and eggs. This diet is said to help nourish the body and eliminate the build-up of toxins. By combining the effects of both the diets, you will have the chance to do your body a whole world of good.

Thanks to this book, you will not have to worry about coming up with vegan recipes of your own, as you can simply go through the recipes mentioned here and put together a meal plan. There are a large variety of recipes to choose from including pastas, soups and salads which are all made using fresh ingredients.

Don't worry about having to incur a large bill for your monthly groceries, as the ingredients mentioned in this book are not expensive. You will be able to make full course meals using the ingredients without exceeding your monthly budget.

What's more, you don't have to worry about running out of recipes as you can always mix and match the ingredients and come up with original recipes of your own. Once you get the hang of it, you will be surprised at your own creative streak. I thank you for choosing this book and hope you have a blast trying out the different recipes mentioned in it!

Chapter 1: Mediterranean Vegan Pastes, Sauces, and Dips

Cilantro Pistou

Prep: 10 min	Total: 15 min	Servings: 6-8

Ingredients:

- 4 cups fresh cilantro leaves

- 1 cup olive oil

- 12 cloves garlic, peeled

- 1 teaspoon salt or to taste

- 1/2 teaspoon freshly ground black pepper

Instructions:

1. Add cilantro, garlic, salt and pepper to a food processor and pulse.

2. While the food processor is running, gently pour oil into it. Blend until smooth.

3. Store in the refrigerator. Can be stored for 2 days.

Tahini Paste

Prep: 2 min	Total: 15 min	Servings: 15

Ingredients:

- 3 cups sesame seeds, hulled

- 6 tablespoons olive oil or more if required

Instructions:

1. Heat a heavy skillet over medium heat. Add

   sesame seeds. Sauté until they are golden brown,

   but be careful not to burn them. Cool completely.

2. Place the sesame seeds into a food processor. Add olive oil. Blend to make a paste. Add more oil if the paste is too thick and blend again.

3. Store in an airtight jar in the refrigerator. It can be stored for many months.

4. This paste is used in making many Mediterranean dishes.

Tahini Sauce

Prep: 5 min	Total: 2 min	Servings: 6

Ingredients:

- 4 cloves garlic, minced
- Salt to taste
- 1 cup tahini paste
- 3/4 cup lemon juice
- 6 tablespoons water

Instructions:

1. Place garlic and salt in a bowl. Mash together the garlic and salt with a mortar and pestle until a paste is made.

2. Transfer into a bowl. Add tahini paste, lemon juice, and water. Whisk until well combined.

3. Refrigerate until use. Can be stored for up to 5 days.

4. Goes well with kebabs.

Bell Pepper, Olive, and Arugula Salsa

Prep: 15 min	Total: 23 min	Servings: 6-8

Ingredients:

- 30 kalamata olives, pitted, quartered

- 1 medium red bell pepper, finely chopped

- 1 medium yellow bell pepper, finely chopped

- 2 teaspoons fennel seeds, crushed

- 1 cup baby arugula, chopped

- 3 tablespoons olive oil

21

Instructions:

1. Place a nonstick pan over medium heat. Add oil. When oil is heated, add fennel seeds and sauté until fragrant.

2. Add bell peppers and sauté until they are soft. Transfer into a bowl.

3. Add salt, pepper and arugula and stir until arugula wilts.

Hummus

Prep: 5 min	Total: 7 min	Servings: 6

Ingredients:

- 2 cups cooked garbanzo beans (chickpeas), retain about 1/2 cup of the cooked liquid

- 2 teaspoons tahini paste

- 2 cloves garlic, crushed

- 1/2 teaspoon sea salt or to taste

- 1 1/2 tablespoons fresh lemon juice

- 3 tablespoons extra virgin olive oil + extra for drizzling
- Pepper to taste
- Paprika to taste (optional)
- Parsley (optional)

Instructions:

1. Blend together all the ingredients, except the olive oil (and paprika and parsley if you are using), along with 1/4 cup of the retained liquid. While the food processor is blending, slowly pour olive oil and blend until smooth. Add more of the retained liquid if required.

2. To serve, pour the hummus in a serving dish and garnish with paprika and parsley. Sprinkle some olive oil on it too.

3. Served with salads, burgers, falafels, raw vegetables, etc.

Lebanese Moutabel

Prep: 15 min	Total: 30 min	Servings: 15

Ingredients:

- 6 medium eggplants

- 8 plum tomatoes, finely chopped

- 4 chili peppers, seeded, finely chopped (optional)

- 8 cloves garlic, minced

- 2 shallots, minced

- 2 cups fresh parsley, chopped

- 2/3 cup extra virgin olive oil

- 1/4 cup lemon juice + extra

- 1 teaspoon ground cumin

- Freshly ground black pepper to taste

- Salt to taste

- Cucumber slices for garnishing

Instructions:

1. Preheat a grill. You can grill on a charcoal grill or roast in an oven.

2. Keep the eggplants directly on the flame or coal and grill until they are well cooked on the inside and charred on the outside. Turn the eggplants around a few times using tongs while cooking.

3. Remove the skin and keep the pulp in a strainer.

4. Meanwhile, mix together tomatoes, chili peppers, garlic, shallots, 1 cup of parsley, half the oil, lemon juice, cumin, pepper and salt. Mix well with the eggplant using a fork.

5. Drizzle the remaining oil. Garnish with remaining parsley and cucumber slices.

Cilantro Garlic Hummus

Prep: 7 min	Total: 10 min	Servings: 6

Ingredients:

- 2 cups hummus
- 2 cups fresh cilantro, chopped
- 10 cloves garlic, peeled
- 2 teaspoons chili flakes
- 2 teaspoons cayenne pepper
- 1 teaspoon rock salt
- 2 tablespoons lemon juice
- 2 teaspoons olive oil

Instructions:

28

1. Place a pan over medium heat. Add oil. When oil is heated, add garlic and sauté for 3-4 minutes.

2. Add chili flakes and cook for a couple of minutes.

3. Cool and add to a blender. Add cilantro, and blend for a minute.

4. Add the rest of the ingredients and blend until smooth.

Avocado Taco Dip Recipe

Prep: 15 min	Total: 17 min	Servings: 12-15

Ingredients:

- 2 ripe avocadoes, peeled, pitted, finely chopped

- 2 cups vegan sour cream

- 4 tablespoons taco seasoning mix

- 2 cups tomatoes, finely chopped

- 2 cups vegan cheddar cheese, shredded

- 1 cup black olives, sliced

Instructions:

1. Add all the ingredients, except olives, to a bowl and mix well.

2. Garnish with olives.

3. Goes well with French bread or tortilla chips.

Baba Ganoush

Prep: 5 min	Total: 25min	Servings: 6

Ingredients:

- 1 large eggplant (about a pound)

- 3 large cloves garlic, unpeeled

- 3 tablespoons lemon juice

- 3 teaspoons tahini paste

- Salt to taste

- Extra virgin olive oil for garnishing

- Sumac powder for garnishing

Instructions:

1. Preheat a grill to a high heat.

2. Meanwhile prick eggplant with a fork. Grill the eggplant until tender on the inside and charred on the outside.

3. Put the garlic onto a skewer. Grill until charred and tender, turning the skewer once.

4. When the eggplant and garlic are cooled, peel the charred skins.

5. Place the eggplant, garlic, lemon juice, tahini and salt in a food processor. Blend until smooth.

6. Transfer into a serving bowl. Sprinkle oil and sumac powder and serve.

Lebanese Muhammara

Prep: 10 min	Total: 40 min	Servings: 12

Ingredients:

- 4 red bell peppers

- 1/2 pound walnuts, toasted + extra to garnish

- 4 tablespoons pomegranate molasses

- 5 tablespoons tomato paste

- 1/2 cup extra virgin olive oil, divided

- 2 cloves garlic, chopped

- 1 1/2 cups breadcrumbs

- 2 teaspoons sumac

- 2 teaspoons red pepper flakes

- 1 teaspoon cayenne pepper or to taste

- 2 teaspoons sugar

- 2 tablespoons fresh parsley, chopped to garnish

Instructions:

1. Lightly coat bell peppers with oil and place in a greased baking dish.

2. Bake in a preheated oven at 425°F for about 30 minutes. Turn the peppers a couple of times while cooking.

3. Transfer into a bowl. Cover and set aside for a while until it cools.

4. Peel, deseed and roughly chop the peppers.

5. Add all the ingredients into a blender and blend until smooth.

6. Garnish with parsley and walnuts and serve at room temperature.

7. Store in an airtight container in the refrigerator. Can be stored for up to 2-3 days.

Chapter 2: Mediterranean Vegan Breakfast Recipes

Focaccia Bread

Prep: 10 min	Total: 60 min	Servings: 4-6

Ingredients:

For dough:

- 1 1/2 cups unbleached, all-purpose flour

- 1/2 cup warm water

- 1/2 teaspoon onion powder

- 1/2 teaspoon dried basil

- 1/2 teaspoon dried oregano

- 1/4 teaspoon dried thyme

- 1/4 teaspoon pepper powder

- 1/2 teaspoon salt

- 1/2 teaspoon agave nectar

- 1 clove garlic, minced

- 2 teaspoons olive oil

- 1/2 tablespoon active dry yeast

  For topping:

- 2 tablespoons sundried tomato, slivered

- 1 teaspoon olive oil

- 3-4 olives, sliced

- 1 small onion, chopped into 1 cm squares

- 1/2 tablespoon fresh rosemary

Instructions:

1. To make dough: Sprinkle yeast over warm water and set aside for 10 minutes.

2. Meanwhile, mix together all the dry ingredients in a large bowl.

3. Add garlic, agave nectar and oil to the warm water.

4. Now, pour this mixture into the bowl of dry ingredients and knead into smooth dough. If you find the dough too dry, then add a little water, a tablespoon at a time, and knead until smooth. If you find it too sticky, add a little more flour a tablespoon at a time.

5. Place the dough in a greased bowl. Cover with a moist towel and set aside in a warm place for 20-30 minutes.

6. Grease a baking sheet and place the dough over it. Roll the dough onto the baking sheet until it is around 1/2-3/4 an inch thick. Press the dough and smoothen the top so that it sticks to the baking sheet.

7. Brush the top with oil. Spread the topping over it. Lightly press it.

8. Bake in a preheated oven at 450°F for 15-18 minutes or until light brown.

9. Remove from oven, cool slightly, slice and serve.

Vegan Shakshouka

Prep: 15 min	Total: 45 min	Servings: 4

Ingredients:

- 1 red bell pepper, chopped

- 4 medium tomatoes, chopped

- 2 packages firm silken tofu, roughly chopped

- 4 cloves garlic, crushed

- 2 onions, chopped

- 2 tablespoons tomato paste

- 2 tablespoons hot sauce

- 2 teaspoons cumin powder

- 1/2 teaspoon turmeric

- 2 teaspoons paprika

- 2 tablespoons olive oil

- 2 tablespoons cornstarch

- 4 tablespoons nutritional yeast

- 2 tablespoons tahini paste or sauce

- 1/2 cup soy milk /almond milk /water

- Salt to taste

- Pepper to taste

- 1 green onion, thinly sliced

- Herbs of your choice to garnish

Instructions:

1. Place a skillet over medium heat. Add oil. When oil is heated, add onions and garlic and sauté until soft.

2. Add spices and salt. Sauté until fragrant then add tomatoes and bell pepper.

3. Cook for a while until the tomatoes begin to turn soft.

4. Add hot sauce, tomato paste and a sprinkle of water and stir-fry for a minute.

5. Lower heat and simmer.

6. Meanwhile, blend together tofu, cornstarch, turmeric, nutritional yeast, soymilk, tahini and salt until smooth and creamy.

7. Transfer the bell pepper mixture into a large, greased baking dish.

8. Spread as much tofu mixture as you desire over it and refrigerate the remaining tofu mixture for the next time.

9. Broil in a preheated oven until the tofu layer is the shade of brown you desire.

10. Garnish with herbs and green onions and serve immediately.

Mediterranean Breakfast Couscous

Prep: 5 min	Total: 25 min	Servings: 4

Ingredients:

- 1 1/2 cups almond or soy milk, unsweetened

- 1-inch cinnamon stick

- 1/2 cup uncooked whole-wheat couscous

- 5 tablespoons chopped dried apricots

- 2 tablespoons dried currants

- 3 teaspoons dark brown sugar, divided or to taste

- 1/8 teaspoon salt

- 2 teaspoons vegan butter, melted, divided

Instructions:

1. Place a saucepan over medium heat. Add soymilk and cinnamon. Heat for a couple of minutes but do not boil.

2. Remove from heat. Add couscous, mix well. Add apricots, currants, brown sugar, and salt.

3. Cover and keep aside for 15 minutes. Discard cinnamon stick. Mix well.

4. Serve in individual bowls topped with butter.

Cheesy Mediterranean Scramble

Prep: 10 min	Total: 25 min	Servings: 6

Ingredients:

- 6 cartons (4 ounces each) egg substitute
- 1/4 cup fat-free vegan feta cheese
- 3 tablespoons vegan butter
- 1 large onion, finely chopped
- 1 large red bell pepper, finely chopped
- 1 teaspoon dried basil, crushed
- Salt to taste
- Pepper to taste

- 12 slices whole wheat bread, toasted

Instructions:

1. Pour egg substitute to a bowl and whisk. Add basil, salt, and pepper and whisk again.

2. Place a large nonstick skillet over medium heat. Add vegan butter. Add red pepper and onion when butter melts.

3. Sauté until onions are translucent. Add egg substitute mixture and stir. Cook until it sets. Stir once in a while.

4. Sprinkle cheese and serve on toast.

Zucchini and Mushroom Frittata

Prep: 10 min	Total: 30 min	Servings: 6-8

Ingredients:

- 2 medium zucchinis, halved lengthwise, thinly sliced

- 16 ounces' mushrooms, sliced

- 1/2 cup onions, finely chopped

- 4 tablespoons vegan butter

- 6 cartons (4 ounces each) cholesterol-free egg substitute

- 2 cloves garlic, minced

- 1 teaspoon fresh thyme leaves, chopped

- Salt to taste

- 1/4 teaspoon ground black pepper

Instructions:

1. Pour egg substitute to a bowl and whisk. Add thyme, salt, and pepper and whisk again.

2. Place a large ovenproof nonstick skillet over medium heat. Add vegan butter. Add mushrooms, zucchini and onion when butter melts.

3. Sauté until onions are translucent. Add garlic and sauté until fragrant.

4. Add egg substitute mixture and stir lightly immediately. Do not stir after this.

5. Cover and cook until it sets.

6. Place the skillet in a preheated oven and broil until the top is golden brown.

7. Slice into wedges and serve.

Mediterranean Quinoa

Prep: 10 min	Total: 30 min	Servings: 4-6

Ingredients:

- 2 cups quinoa, cook according to instructions on the package
- 1 1/2 cups sun dried tomatoes, thinly sliced
- 1 1/2 cups roasted peppers, thinly sliced
- 30 kalamata olives, pitted, quartered
- 1 1/2 cups artichoke hearts, thinly sliced
- 1 tablespoon lemon juice
- 10 cloves garlic, minced
- 1/2 cup basil, thinly sliced

- Salt to taste

- Pepper powder to taste

Instructions:

1. Add all the ingredients to a bowl and toss well.

2. Serve as it is or chill and serve later.

Italian Scramble

Prep: 10 min	Total: 20 min	Servings: 4

Ingredients:

- 1 1/2 packages tofu, crumbled

- 1 large onion, chopped

- 1 green chili, thinly sliced

- 1 small green bell pepper, chopped

- 1 small red bell pepper, chopped

- 1 small yellow bell pepper, chopped

- 4 cloves garlic, minced

- 2 tablespoons olive oil

- 2 tablespoons Italian seasoning or to taste

- 1 1/2 teaspoons crushed red pepper flakes

- 1 teaspoon turmeric powder

- 3 cups spinach, rinsed, chopped

- 1 1/2 cups cherry tomatoes

- 4 tablespoons capers

- 1 1/2 teaspoons sea salt or to taste

Instructions:

1. Place a skillet over medium heat. Add oil. When the oil is heated, add onions and bell peppers and sauté until the vegetables are soft.

2. Add turmeric and Italian seasoning and sauté for a few seconds.

3. Add spinach, green chili, and tomatoes and sauté for a few minutes until spinach wilts.

4. Add tofu and capers, mix well and heat thoroughly. Taste and adjust the seasonings if necessary.

5. Remove from heat and serve.

Cioccolata Calda (Italian Hot Chocolate)

Prep: 5 min	Total: 10 min	Servings: 2

Ingredients:

- 4 tablespoons cocoa powder, unsweetened

- 1 1/2 cups almond

- 1/4 cup cashew milk

- 4 teaspoons cornstarch

- 4 tablespoons granulated sugar

- 1/2 teaspoon vanilla extract

Instructions:

1. Add all the ingredients, except cornstarch, vanilla and cashew milk, to a blender and blend until smooth. Pour into a large saucepan.

2. Place the saucepan over medium heat. Bring to a simmer, stirring frequently.

3. Whisk together in a small bowl, cornstarch and cashew milk. Pour this mixture into the saucepan, stirring constantly.

4. Reduce heat and simmer until thick.

5. Remove from heat and add vanilla extract.

6. Mix well, pour into cups and serve.

Chapter 3: Mediterranean Vegan Salad Recipes

Minty Winter Tabbouleh

Prep: 10 min	Total: 30 min	Servings: 4

Ingredients:

- 6 tablespoons bulgur, cook according to instructions on the package
- 1 small onion, minced
- 1 cup tightly packed parsley, minced
- 1 cup tightly packed fresh peppermint leaves, minced

- 1/2 teaspoon garlic, minced

- 3 tablespoons hazelnuts, chopped, toasted

- 1 cucumber, chopped

- 3 sundried tomatoes in oil, rinsed, pat dried

- 2 tablespoons oil from sundried tomatoes

- 2 tablespoons lemon juice

- Salt to taste

- Pepper to taste

Instructions:

1. Add all ingredients to a bowl and toss well. Chill for at least an hour and serve.

Greek Salad

Prep: 10 min	Total: 12 min	Servings: 6

Ingredients:

- 10-12 ripe cherry tomatoes
- 2 medium ripe tomatoes, chopped into wedges
- 1 large red onion, peeled, very thinly sliced
- 2 cucumbers, cut into thick slices
- 2 green peppers, deseeded, sliced into rings
- 1/2 cup fresh dill, chopped + extra for garnishing
- 1/2 cup fresh mint leaves, chopped + extra for garnishing
- 1/2 cup, black olives, pitted, sliced

- Sea salt to taste

- 2 tablespoons red wine vinegar

- 6 tablespoons Greek extra virgin olive oil

- 1 cup vegan fat-free feta cheese, crumbled

- 2 teaspoons oregano

Instructions

1. Mix together all the ingredients, except oil,

   cheese and oregano, in a large bowl. Toss well.

2. Sprinkle olive oil, cheese and oregano on top and

   serve immediately.

Big Italian salad

Prep: 15 min	Total: 20 min	Servings: 4

Ingredients:

Dressing:

- 2 cups fresh Italian parsley, loosely packed

- 20-25 big leaves of basil

- 1/2 teaspoon dried oregano

- 4 cloves garlic, peeled

- 1/2 cup red wine vinegar

- 1 cup extra virgin olive oil

- 1 1/2 teaspoon salt or to taste

- 1/2 teaspoon pepper

- 3 teaspoons agave nectar

Salad:

- 1 large head romaine lettuce, washed, chopped

- 1 small head radicchio, halved, cored, chopped

- 1 small head iceberg lettuce, chopped

- 1 large bell pepper, chopped

- 1 hothouse cucumber, sliced

- 2 carrots, halved, thinly sliced

- 1 cup cherry tomatoes, halved

- Half cup green olives, pitted

- 1 cup vegan ricotta

Instructions:

1. Mix together all the ingredients of the salad in a large bowl.

2. Blend together all the ingredients of the dressing in a blender until smooth.

3. Pour about half the dressing over the salad and toss, taste and add more dressing if required.

Lebanese Fattoush

Prep: 15 min	Total: 30 min	Servings: 4

Ingredients:

- 1 (6-inch) whole-wheat pita bread, split

- 2 tablespoons extra-virgin olive oil, divided

- 3/4 teaspoon ground sumac, divided

- 2 tablespoons lemon juice

- 1/4 teaspoon salt or to taste

- Freshly ground pepper to taste

- 1 medium head romaine lettuce, chopped

- 1 large tomato, chopped

- 1 small cucumber, chopped

- 1 small red onion, thinly sliced

- 1 tablespoon fresh mint, thinly chopped

Instructions:

1. Place the pita halves on a baking sheet with the rough side up. Brush about 1/2 tablespoon olive oil and sprinkle half the sumac over it.

2. Bake in a preheated oven at 350°F for about 15 minutes or until crisp and golden. When cool enough to handle, chop into bite-size pieces.

3. In a glass bowl add lemon juice, salt, pepper, remaining oil and sumac. Whisk well. Add the rest of the ingredients and the pita pieces.

4. Toss well to coat.

5. Serve after 15 minutes.

Mediterranean Salad

Prep: 15 min	Total: 30 min	Servings: 2-3

Ingredients:

For salad:

- 2 Persian cucumbers, chopped

- 1 small green bell pepper, deseeded, chopped

- 2 -3 radishes, chopped

- 2 tomatoes, chopped

- 2 green onions, sliced

- 1 dill pickle, chopped

    For dressing:

- 2 tablespoons extra virgin olive oil

- 1/2 teaspoon garlic powder

- Juice of 1/2 lemon

- Salt to taste

- Pepper to taste

Instructions:

1. Add dressing ingredients to a bowl and whisk well.

2. Add rest of the ingredients and toss well.

3. Refrigerate for 15 minutes. Toss again and serve.

Moroccan Carrot and Chickpea Salad

Prep: 15 min	Total: 20 min	Servings: 2-3

Ingredients:

Dressing:

- 2 tablespoons extra virgin olive oil

- 1/2 teaspoon lemon zest, grated

- 2 tablespoons lemon juice

- 2 tablespoons fresh orange juice

- 3/4 tablespoon agave nectar

- Salt to taste

- 1/2 teaspoon ground cumin

- 1/2 teaspoon ground ginger

- 1/4 teaspoon ground cinnamon

- 1/4 teaspoon ground coriander

- 1/4 teaspoon ground all spice

- 1/4 teaspoon cayenne pepper

Salad:

- 3/4 pound carrots, peeled, grated

- 3 tablespoon currants

- 1/4 cup almonds, slivered, toasted OR walnuts, chopped

- 2 tablespoons fresh cilantro, chopped

- 2 tablespoons fresh mint, chopped

- 1/2 a 15 ounces can chickpeas, rinsed, drained

- 1 tablespoon shallots, minced

- 2 cloves garlic, minced

Instructions:

1. Mix all the ingredients of the salad in a large bowl.

2. In a small bowl, whisk together all the ingredients of the dressing.

3. Pour the dressing over the salad. Toss. Cover and refrigerate until use.

Chapter 4: Mediterranean Vegan Soup Recipes

Giouvarlakia (Greek Meatball Soup)

Prep: 10 min	Total: 60 min	Servings: 4

Ingredients:

- 3/4 cup dry brown lentils, rinsed, soaked in water for a couple of hours if possible

- 2 tablespoons breadcrumbs

- 7 tablespoons long grain brown rice

- 1/4 cup flour

- 1 small onion, chopped

- 3 cups vegetable broth

- 1/2 tablespoon cornstarch mixed with 2 tablespoons water

- 2 tablespoons parsley, chopped

- 1 tablespoon olive oil

- 1 tablespoon ground flaxseeds

- Salt to taste

- Pepper to taste

- Juice of a lemon

- 2 cups water

Instructions:

1. Place a saucepan with 2 cups broth and lentils over medium high heat and bring to a boil.

2. Reduce heat and simmer until lentils are cooked. Strain lentils and retain cooked water

3. Place another small saucepan with 6 tablespoons rice and remaining broth, and cook until rice is cooked.

4. Add the retained liquid back into the saucepan. Also add water and place over medium heat.

5. Meanwhile, add lentils and half the cooked rice to a blender and pulse until coarsely mashed.

6. Transfer into a large bowl. Add remaining cooked rice, parsley, oil, breadcrumbs and flaxseeds and mix until well combined.

7. Divide the mixture and shape into 10-12 small balls.

8. Add remaining tablespoon of uncooked rice to the broth and lower the lentil balls into it.

9. Reduce heat and simmer for about 30 minutes.

10. Add cornstarch mixture to the simmering broth and stir gently. Add lemon juice, salt and pepper.

11. Serve hot in bowls. Drizzle a little olive oil if you desire.

Mediterranean Stew

Prep: 20 min	Total: 60 min	Servings: 6-8

Ingredients:

- 1/2 butternut squash, peeled, deseeded, cubed

- 1 cup eggplant, cubed

- 1 cup zucchini, cubed

- 1/2 a 10-ounce package frozen okra, thawed

- 1/2 an 8 ounces can tomato sauce

- 1/2 a 15 ounces can chickpeas, drained, rinsed

- 1/2 cup onions, chopped

- 1/2 cup mushrooms, sliced

78

- 2 cloves garlic, minced

- 1 tomato, chopped

- 1 carrot, thinly sliced

- 1 small bell pepper, chopped

- 1/2 cup low sodium vegetable broth

- 1 tablespoon olive oil

- 3 tablespoons raisins

- A large pinch cinnamon powder

- 1/4 teaspoon turmeric powder

- Red chili flakes to taste

- 1/4 teaspoon cumin powder

- A large pinch paprika

- 2 tablespoons parsley, chopped to garnish

Instructions:

1. Place a skillet over medium heat with oil. When oil is heated, add onion and pepper and sauté for a couple of minutes. Add spices and sauté for a few seconds until fragrant.

2. Add eggplant, garlic, mushrooms and sauté for about 5-7 minutes. Add rest of the ingredients and simmer until the vegetables are cooked.

3. Garnish with parsley and serve in bowls.

Egyptian Red Lentil Soup

Prep: 15 min	Total: 45 min	Servings: 6

Ingredients:

- 1 1/2 cups red lentils

- 5 cups water

- 1 carrot, sliced

- 1 medium onion, chopped

- 2 Roma tomatoes, chopped

- 6 cloves garlic, chopped

- 1/2 cube vegetarian bouillon

- 3 teaspoons ground cumin

- 1/2 teaspoon ground coriander

- 1 teaspoon salt

- 3/4 teaspoon freshly cracked black pepper

Instructions:

1. Place a saucepan with 4 cups water, lentils, tomatoes, carrot, onion, garlic and bouillon over a medium heat.

2. Cook until lentils are tender.

3. Remove from heat and cool for a while. Blend the entire mixture with an immersion blender.

4. Add cumin, salt, pepper and coriander to the remaining cup of water and add it to the blended soup. Stir well and heat thoroughly.

5. Serve hot in bowls.

Mediterranean Bean Soup

Prep: 10 min	Total: 55 min	Servings: 8

Ingredients:

- 2 medium onions, chopped

- 1 1/2 tablespoons olive oil

- 4 cloves garlic, crushed

- 2 bay leaves

- 2 medium carrots, sliced

- 1 1/2 cans (15 ounces each) dark red kidney beans

- 1 1/2 cans (15 ounces each) tomato sauce

- 1 1/2 cans (15 ounces each) cannellini beans

- 6 cups vegetable broth

- 3/4 cup red wine

- 3 tablespoons dried parsley

- 1 teaspoon dried oregano

- 1 1/2 teaspoons dried thyme

- Salt to taste

- Pepper powder to taste

Instructions:

1. Place a pot over medium heat. Add oil. When oil is heated, add onions and carrots and sauté until onions are translucent.

2. Add garlic and sauté until fragrant. Add rest of the ingredients and bring to a boil.

3. Lower heat and simmer for about 25-30 minutes.

84

4. Ladle into individual soup bowls and serve.

Italian Wedding Soup

Prep: min	Total: min	Servings: 4

Ingredients:

- 1/2 cup onions, finely chopped

- 2 tablespoons olive oil

- 1 medium carrot, chopped

- 2 stalks celery, chopped

- 1 whole clove garlic, peeled

- 1 teaspoon garlic, minced

- 1/3 cup ditalini pasta

- 2.5 ounces' fresh spinach, chopped

- 4 cups vegetable broth

- 1/2 tablespoon dried oregano

- 1/2 tablespoon dried parsley

- 1/2 tablespoon dried basil

- 1 tablespoon lemon juice

- Salt to taste

- Pepper to taste

Instructions:

1. Place a pot over medium heat with a tablespoon of oil. When oil is hot, add onions and garlic and sauté until translucent.

2. Add carrots and celery and sauté for 4-5 minutes. Add dried spices and sauté for a few seconds.

3. Lower heat, add pasta and simmer for 10 minutes. Lower the meatballs into it and continue simmering.

4. Meanwhile, place a skillet over medium heat. Add a tablespoon of oil. When oil is heated, add whole clove of garlic and crush it simultaneously as it cooks. Add spinach and cook until spinach wilts. Transfer into the pot. Add lemon juice, salt and pepper and heat thoroughly.

5. Ladle into individual soup bowls and serve.

Zuppa Vegana

Prep: 15 min	Total: 50 min	Servings: 8

Ingredients:

- 1 cup onions, chopped
- 1/2 pound small potatoes, chopped into bite-size pieces
- 6 cups kale leaves, chopped, discard hard stems and ribs
- 4 cloves garlic, minced
- 1 can (15 ounces) pinto beans (drain off and dry)
- 5 cups vegetable broth

- 1/2 teaspoon dried basil

- 1/2 teaspoon dried oregano

- 1/4 teaspoon dried rosemary, crushed

- 1/4 teaspoons red pepper flakes

- 1/4 teaspoon fennel seeds

- 1/4 cup non-dairy milk

- 1 tablespoon nutritional yeast

Instructions:

1. Place a large pot or saucepan over medium heat. Add onions and a tablespoon of water and sauté until onions turn soft. Add garlic and sauté for a minute.

2. Add rest of the ingredients, except kale, milk and nutritional yeast, and bring to a boil.

3. Lower heat, cover, and cook until the potatoes are tender.

4. Add kale, cover, and cook for 5-8 minutes until kale is bright green and tender.

5. Remove about half of the soup, blend with a hand blender and pour it back to the pot.

6. Reheat. Taste and adjust the seasonings if necessary.

7. Add milk and nutritional yeast. Mix well.

Avgolemano (Greek Easter Soup)

Prep: 10 min	Total: 50 min	Servings: 3-4

Ingredients:

- 1/2 cup long grain brown rice, soaked in water for an hour
- 2 teaspoons olive oil
- 1 shallot, chopped
- 1 small onion, chopped
- 1 medium carrot, chopped
- 1 large clove garlic, minced
- 1 stalk celery, chopped
- 4 cups low-sodium vegetable broth

- 2 teaspoons white miso

- 2 tablespoons lemon juice

- 1/2 teaspoon salt

- 1 tablespoon tahini paste

- 3 tablespoons fresh dill, chopped

- 2 tablespoons nutritional yeast

Instructions:

1. Place a pot over medium heat. Add oil. When oil is heated, add onions and sauté until translucent. Add shallots, carrot and celery and sauté until tender.

2. Add garlic and sauté until fragrant. Sprinkle water if getting stuck.

3. Add rice and sauté for a couple of minutes. Add broth and salt and bring to a boil.

4. Lower heat and simmer until rice is cooked.

5. Mix together in a bowl, lemon juice, miso, and tahini with 1/4 cup of the simmering soup. Pour into the pot and stir. Add nutritional yeast and simmer for a couple of minutes.

6. Add dill and simmer for another 2 minutes.

7. Ladle into soup bowls and serve immediately.

Lebanese Lentil Soup

Prep: 15 min	Total: 50 min	Servings: 6

Ingredients:

- 1 cup red or brown lentils, picked, rinsed, soaked in water for an hour if possible
- 1 1/2 tablespoons olive oil
- 3 cloves garlic, minced
- 1 large onion, finely chopped
- 1 cup spinach, chopped
- 1/2 teaspoon cayenne pepper

- 1 teaspoon ground cumin

- 2 tablespoons lemon juice

- Zest of 1/2 lemon

- 2 tablespoons fresh mint, chopped

- Salt to taste

- Freshly cracked pepper to taste

Instructions:

1. Place a large pot over medium heat. Add oil and onions and sauté until translucent.

2. Lower heat and cook until onions are light brown.

3. Add garlic and sauté until fragrant. Add spices and stir. Add lentils and water and bring to a boil.

4. Lower heat and simmer until lentils are cooked.

5. Add mint, salt and pepper. Remove a little of the cooked lentils, mash and add it back to the pot.

6. Add spinach and cook until it wilts. Add lemon juice, zest, salt and pepper and simmer for a couple of minutes.

7. Ladle into soup bowls and serve.

French Onion Soup

Prep: 15 min	Total: 45 min	Servings: 4

Ingredients:

- 2 cups onions, sliced

- 1 tablespoon vegan butter

- 6 tablespoons red wine or sherry

- 4 cups vegetable stock

- 2 sprigs thyme

- Salt to taste

- Freshly ground pepper to taste

- 1/2 tablespoon balsamic vinegar

- 1 bay leaf

- 1/2 cup vegan mozzarella or cheddar cheese

- 3 sprigs flat leaf parsley

- A few croutons to serve

Instructions:

1. Place a pot over medium high heat. Add butter, onions, salt and pepper and sauté for about 5 minutes. Stir frequently.

2. Add wine and vinegar and simmer for 5-7 minutes. Add stock, spices, and herbs and simmer for 15 minutes.

3. Ladle into soup bowls. Top with croutons and cheese and serve.

Moroccan Lentil Soup

Prep: 10 min	Total: 55 min	Servings: 4

Ingredients:

- 1 onion, chopped

- 2 cloves garlic, minced

- 1/2 teaspoon fresh ginger, grated

- 4 cups water or vegetable stock

- 1/2 cup green lentils

- 1/2 a 15 ounces can garbanzo beans, drained

- 1/2 cup quinoa

- 1/2 a 14.5 ounce can diced tomatoes

99

- 1/2 cup carrots, diced

- 1/4 cup celery

- 3/4 teaspoon ground cinnamon

- 1/4 teaspoon ground nutmeg

- 1/4 teaspoon cayenne pepper

- 1 teaspoon paprika

- 1/4 teaspoon saffron threads

- 1/4 teaspoon ground cumin

- 1/2 tablespoon olive oil

- 2 tablespoons fresh cilantro, chopped

- 2 tablespoons fresh parsley, chopped

- 2 tablespoons lemon juice

- Salt to taste

- Pepper to taste

Instructions:

1. Place a large pot with olive oil over medium heat. Add onions, garlic and ginger. Sauté until the onions are translucent.

2. Add rest of the ingredients and bring to a boil.

3. Lower heat and simmer for about an hour or until the lentils are cooked.

4. Remove half the soup from the pot. Cool a little and blend with a stick blender.

5. Transfer the puréed soup back to the pot. Mix well, reheat and serve.

Chapter 4: Mediterranean Vegan Appetizers Recipes

Greek Fava

Prep: min	Total: min	Servings:

Ingredients:

- 2 cups santorini fava (yellow split peas), rinsed

- 4 tablespoons olive oil

- 2 large onions, chopped

- 1 teaspoon salt

  To garnish:

- Lemon juice as required

- Extra virgin olive oil as required

- 2 spring onions, thinly sliced

- 2 tablespoons capers

Instructions:

1. Place fava in a large pot. Cover with water and bring to a boil. It will start getting frothy. Remove froth, drain fava and rinse again.

2. Add the fava back to the pot. Add 5 cups water and bring to a boil.

3. Reduce heat and simmer. Add onions, oil and salt and cook until fava is tender. If it is too dry, then add more water.

4. Remove from heat and cool. Blend with an immersion blender until creamy.

5. Ladle into small plates. Drizzle oil and lemon juice over it. Sprinkle capers and spring onions and serve.

Mediterranean Stuffed Mushrooms

Prep: 10 min	Total: 40 min	Servings: 6-8

Ingredients:

- 2 dozen button mushroom caps, discard stems
- 1/2 cup vegan feta cheese, crumbled
- 2 cans whole artichoke hearts, drained
- 4 tablespoons olive oil, divided
- 2 teaspoons lemon zest, grated

- 1 teaspoon dried Mediterranean herbs or Herbes de Provence
- 1/2 teaspoon freshly ground pepper
- Salt to taste

Instructions:

1. Grease a baking dish with a teaspoon of oil. Place the mushrooms in the dish with their stem sides up.

2. Slice the artichoke heart leaves and stuff them inside the mushrooms. Sprinkle feta, lemon zest, pepper and dried herbs over mushrooms. Drizzle the remaining oil over them.

3. Bake in a preheated oven for about 30 minutes.

4. Put toothpicks in the mushrooms and serve.

Italian Bruschetta with Sautéed Mushrooms

Prep: 15 min	Total: 35 min	Servings: 4-5

Ingredients:

- A few slices vegan Italian bread, toasted

- 1 tablespoon garlic, sliced

- 4 cups mixed mushrooms of your choice, chopped

- 1 large handful fresh thyme leaves, chopped

- 2 handfuls flat leaf parsley leaves, chopped

- 5 tablespoons extra virgin olive oil + extra if required

- Salt to taste

- Pepper powder to taste

Instructions:

1. Place a skillet over medium heat. Add half the oil. When oil is heated, add garlic and sauté until garlic is fragrant.

2. Add mushrooms, salt and pepper and sauté until mushrooms are soft. Remove from heat and cool for a while. Stir on and off.

3. Add parsley and thyme and cook for about 5 minutes.

4. Remove from heat.

5. To serve: Place cooked mushrooms over toasted bread slices. Season with salt and pepper. Drizzle a little olive oil over them and serve.

Spanish Patatas Bravas

Prep: 10 min	Total: 40min	Servings: 4

Ingredients:

- 3/4 pound red potatoes, chopped into 1-inch-thick wedges
- 1/3 cup canned crushed tomatoes
- 2 tablespoons olive oil, divided
- 1/2 teaspoon hot smoked paprika
- 2 teaspoons garlic, minced

Instructions:

1. Place potatoes on a baking sheet and sprinkle a tablespoon of oil over them. Toss and sprinkle salt and pepper.

2. Bake in a preheated oven at 425°F until golden brown. Flip sides and bake for another 8-10 minutes until golden brown. Sprinkle half the garlic over them, mix and transfer into a bowl.

3. Meanwhile, make the sauce as follows: Place a saucepan with remaining oil in it over medium heat. Add remaining garlic and sauté until fragrant.

4. Add paprika, salt, pepper, and tomatoes and simmer until the sauce thickens.

109

5. Serve with the roasted potatoes.

Lebanese Shish Taouk (Vegan Shish Kebabs)

Prep: 10 min	Total: 20 min	Servings: 6

Ingredients:

For marinade:

- 1/2 cup plain vegan yogurt

- 4 tablespoons tomato paste

- 6 tablespoons lemon juice

- 6 tablespoons olive oil

110

- 2 tablespoons paprika

- 1 teaspoon ground cumin

- 1 1/2 teaspoons dried thyme

- 1/2 teaspoon allspice

- 8 cloves garlic, minced

- Salt to taste

- Pepper to taste

  For kebabs:

- 16 ounces' tempeh or 28 ounces' firm tofu, cubed

- 1 large green bell pepper, chopped into 1 inch squares

- 1 large red bell pepper, chopped into 1 inch squares

- 1 onion, quartered, leaves separated

111

- Cooking spray

- Bamboo skewers soaked in water for 30 minutes just before grilling

Instructions:

1. Mix together all the ingredients of the marinade in a bowl. Add tempeh or tofu and mix well.

2. Cover and refrigerate for at least 4 hours.

3. Thread the tofu or tempeh on the skewers alternating with onions and peppers.

4. Grill in a preheated grill on medium heat. Spray with cooking spray.

5. Turn the kebabs around so that they brown on all sides. Serve hot.

Chapter 5: Mediterranean Vegan Main Course

Greek Spetsofai

Prep: 20 min	Total: 55 min	Servings: 4-6

Ingredients:

- 2 big vegan sausages, sliced

- 1 medium onion, thinly sliced

- 3 tablespoons olive oil

- 3 cloves garlic, sliced

- 2 spring onions, thinly sliced

- 1 green bell pepper, chopped into wedges

- 1 ripe tomato, grated

- 1 medium carrot, sliced

- 3 tablespoons red wine

- 1/4 teaspoon chili powder

- 1/2 teaspoon sweet paprika

- A pinch sugar

- Salt to taste

- Pepper to taste

Instructions:

1. Place a skillet over medium-high heat. Add half the oil. When oil is heated, add sausages and sauté for a couple of minutes. Remove and place on a plate.

2. Place the skillet back on heat. Add remaining oil, onions, garlic, peppers and carrot and sauté until vegetables are soft.

3. Add wine and stir.

4. Reduce heat. Add tomatoes, spices and sugar and continue cooking for a few minutes.

5. Add sausages and simmer for about 20 minutes. Add water if required.

6. Serve with lightly toasted bread.

Mujadara with Lebanese Salata

Prep: 10 min	Total: 40 min	Servings: 3-4

Ingredients:

For mujadara:

- 1 to 2 large onions, sliced

- 1 cup lentils, rinsed

- 1 1/2 tablespoons lentils, rinsed

- 1/2 cup brown rice

- 2 cups vegetable broth

- 1 teaspoon ground cumin

- 1/4 cup water or more if required

- Salt to taste

- Cooking spray

  For Lebanese salata:

- 1 medium tomato, chopped

- 1/2 bunch scallions, chopped

- 1 medium English cucumber, chopped

- 4 teaspoons red wine vinegar

- 4 teaspoons olive oil

- Coarse sea salt to taste

Instructions:

1. For mujadara: Add all the ingredients of mujadara, except onions, to a saucepan and cook until tender. Stir occasionally.

2. Meanwhile, place a nonstick pan over medium heat. Spray liberally with cooking spray. Add onions and sauté until golden brown.

3. Transfer the cooked rice-lentil mixture into the pan and mix well. Remove from heat.

4. To make Lebanese salata: Add all the ingredients of the salata to a bowl and toss well.

5. Place salata over mujadara and serve.

Spanish Paella Primavera

Prep: 15 min	Total: 30 min	Servings: 8-10

Ingredients:

- 1 1/2 cups short grain white rice

- 4 1/2 cups vegetable broth

- 1 1/2 tablespoons olive oil

- 1 1/2 cups green onions, thinly sliced

- 1 1/2 cups red bell pepper, chopped

- 1 1/2 tablespoons garlic, minced

- 4 1/2 cup broccoli florets or zucchini, chopped

- 1 1/2 cups grape or cherry tomatoes, halved

- 1 1/2 cups green peas, fresh or frozen

- 15 black olives, halved

- 15 green olives, halved

- 1/3 cup fresh parsley, chopped

- 1 1/2 teaspoons saffron threads, crumbled

- Salt to taste

- Pepper to taste

- Lemon wedges to serve

Instructions:

1. Place a large nonstick skillet over medium heat. Add oil. When oil is heated, add bell pepper and green onions and sauté for 4-5 minutes.

2. Add garlic, broth and saffron and bring to a boil.

3. Add rice and mix well.

4. Lower heat till medium-low, cover and cook for about 10 minutes.

5. Sprinkle broccoli, peas, tomatoes, salt, pepper, and olives over the rice. Do not stir.

6. Cover and cook until rice is tender.

7. Remove from heat and set aside covered for 5-10 minutes.

8. Garnish with parsley and serve with lemon wedges.

Cauliflower Shawarma

Prep: 15 min	Total: 45 min	Servings: 6

Ingredients:

For shwarma spice blend:

- 2 teaspoons garlic powder

- 2 teaspoons ground coriander

- 2 teaspoons ground cumin

- 1 teaspoon paprika

- 1/2 teaspoon ground cinnamon

- 1/2 teaspoon ground pepper

- 1/2 teaspoon ground cardamom

- 1/8 teaspoon ground nutmeg

- 1/4 teaspoon ground cloves

- 1/4 teaspoon ground allspice

  For cauliflower shwarma:

- 1 large head cauliflower, chopped into florets

- 1 teaspoon cayenne

- 1/2 cup water

- 4 teaspoons oil

- 1 teaspoon salt

- 2 teaspoons garlic paste

  To serve:

- Pita bread as required, warmed

- 1 medium cucumber, chopped

- 1 large tomato, chopped

- Lettuce leaves as required, chopped

- Tahini sauce as required

- Hummus as required

- Fresh cilantro, chopped

Instructions:

1. To make shwarma spice blend: Mix together all the ingredients of the spice blend and set aside (use as much as required).

2. To make shwarma: Place a large skillet over medium heat and add cauliflower, water and salt. Cover and cook until al dente.

3. Add about 5-6 teaspoons of the blended spices to oil in a bowl. Add garlic, salt, and cayenne. Pour this mixture over the cauliflower and toss well.

4. Cook for 2-3 minutes until fragrant. Taste and adjust the seasonings if necessary.

5. Spread a generous amount of hummus over the pita. Place cauliflower, tomatoes, cucumber and lettuce on top.

6. Dot with tahini sauce all over. Sprinkle cilantro and serve.

7. You can fill this inside the pita too and serve.

Syrian Mehshi Jazzar

Prep: 10 min	Total: 1 hr 45 min	Servings: 4-5

Ingredients:

For stuffing:

- 1/2 cup brown rice

- 2 cloves garlic, sliced

- 1/4 cup onion, chopped

- 10 small, fat carrots (4 inches each) peeled, trimmed

- 1 tablespoon mint, chopped

- 1 tablespoon parsley, chopped

- 1 tablespoon dill, chopped

127

- 1 tablespoon olive oil

- 3/4 cup water

- 1/2 teaspoon ground cumin

- 1/4 teaspoon ground cinnamon

- 1/4 teaspoon ground allspice

- 1 teaspoon salt or to taste

  For sauce:

- 4 ounces' tomato sauce

- 1 sweet potato, peeled, sliced into 1/2-inch-thick
  pieces

- 2 tablespoons tamarind sauce

- 1 tablespoon sugar

- 1 cup water

- 6 dried apricots, sliced

- 1 tablespoon mint, chopped

- Juice of 1/2 lemon

Instructions:

1. Place a skillet over medium heat. Add oil. When oil is heated, add onions and garlic and sauté until onions are translucent.

2. Add water and bring to a boil. Add salt and rice and cook until rice is tender.

3. Add herbs and spices to mix. Remove from heat and cool completely.

4. Place a pot of water over medium heat. Add carrots and parboil it. Remove with a slotted spoon and set aside until cool.

5. Leave the bottom of the carrots intact and core the carrots. Stuff the rice mixture into the carrots and set aside.

6. To make sauce: Add tomato sauce, water, tamarind, lemon, sugar and mint to a saucepan and place the saucepan over medium heat. Bring to a boil.

7. Grease a baking dish or a roaster with oil. Place the sweet potato slices in a single layer. Overlap if necessary.

8. Place carrots over the sweet potatoes. Place the apricots in between the carrots.

9. Pour sauce over the carrots.

10. Bake in a preheated oven until nearly dry.

Egyptian Koshari

Prep: 30 min	Total: min	Servings: 4

Ingredients:

- 1 cup cooked elbow pasta or shell pasta

- 1 cup cooked rice

- 1 1/2 cups cooked brown lentils

- 2 cans (6 ounces each) tomato paste

- 1 1/2 cups water

- 8 ounces' frozen spinach, chopped

- 2 tablespoons sugar

- 4 cloves garlic, minced

- 2 tablespoons vinegar

131

- 1/2 teaspoon cayenne

- 1 teaspoon ground cumin

- Salt to taste

- French fried crispy onions to serve

Instructions:

1. Mix together rice, pasta, lentils and spinach.

2. Add rest of the ingredients, except onion rings, to a pan and place over medium heat. Bring to a boil and remove from heat.

3. Add sauce to the rice mixture. Mix well and place on a serving dish.

4. Top with French fried onions and serve.

Lebanese Moussaka

Prep: 15 min	Total: 50 min	Servings: 8

Ingredients:

- 6 medium eggplants (about 3 pounds), chopped into 1.5 inch cubes

- 4 large onions, sliced

- 2 large green bell peppers, chopped into chunks

- 2 medium-sized garlic heads

- 4 large tomatoes, chopped into chunks

- 3/4 cup olive oil

- Salt to taste

- 1/2 teaspoon cayenne pepper

- Pita bread to serve

Instructions:

1. Place a large skillet or pot over medium heat. Add oil. When oil is heated, add onions and eggplants and sauté for about 5-6 minutes.

2. Add garlic and bell pepper and stir.

3. Reduce heat and simmer for 10 minutes.

4. Add tomatoes, cayenne pepper and stir.

5. Cover and simmer for 20 minutes. Stir a couple of times while cooking.

6. Remove from heat and cool completely.

7. Serve cold with pita bread.

Chapter 6: Mediterranean Vegan Dessert Recipes

Mediterranean Halva Pudding

Prep: 10 min	Total: 30 min	Servings: 8

Ingredients:

For pudding:

- 1 cup coarse semolina

- 3 tablespoons olive oil

- 1/3 cup mixed nuts, chopped (almond, pistachio and cashew) + extra for garnishing

- 1/2 teaspoon ground cinnamon

For syrup:

- 2 1/4 cups water

- 1 cup sugar

- 2 tablespoons brandy

- 1/4 cup orange juice

- 1/2 cup agave nectar or maple syrup or (honey if you use)

- 1 stick cinnamon

- 3 whole cloves

Instructions:

1. To make syrup: Add all the ingredients of the syrup to a saucepan and place over medium heat. Bring to a boil. Lower heat and simmer for 5 minutes. Remove from heat, cover and set aside.

2. Place a pan with oil over medium heat. Add
    semolina and stir well.

3. Lower heat and roast until light brown in color.
    Stir frequently.

4. Add nuts and roast for another 3-4 minutes.

5. Pour the syrup into the pan, stirring
    simultaneously. Cook until almost dry.

6. Remove from heat, cover and set aside for 10
    minutes.

7. Transfer halva into moulds and let it set (a couple
    of hours)

8. To serve, invert on to a plate. Sprinkle cinnamon
    and nuts and serve.

Spanish Sangria Dessert

Prep: 10 min	Total: 60 min	Servings: 6

Ingredients:

- 1/2 package lemon gelatin, sugar free

- 1/2 package raspberry gelatin

- 1/2 cup boiling water

- 1/2 cup cold water

- 1/2 cup white wine

- 1/2 11 ounces can mandarin oranges, drained

- 1/2 cup fresh raspberries

- 1/2 cup green grapes, halved

Instructions

1. Place boiling water in a large bowl. Add both the gelatins. Stir and dissolve the gelatins. Keep aside for 10 minutes.

2. Add cold water and stir well. Add wine and stir again.

3. Place in the refrigerator for 45 minutes or until slightly set.

4. Add oranges, raspberries, and grapes. Fold gently. Pour into wine glasses. Place in the refrigerator until it sets.

5. Serve chilled.

Italian Castagnaccio (Chestnut Cake)

Prep: 5 min	Total: 45 min	Servings: 10

Ingredients:

- 3 cups chestnut flour

- 3 cups water

- 2 tablespoons coconut sugar or fine caster sugar

- 4 tablespoons extra virgin olive oil

- 1 cup raisins

- 1/4 cup pine nuts

- 1/4 cup walnuts

- 1/8 teaspoon salt

- 2 large sprigs of rosemary (use leaves only).

- Maple syrup or agave nectar as required

Instructions:

1. Add chestnut flour, sugar, salt and half the water to a bowl and whisk. After this, add a tablespoon of water at a time and whisk until smooth. Remember that the batter should be smooth and dropping?? consistency but not runny.

2. Add half the raisins to the batter and fold.

3. Grease 2 pie dishes with a little oil and place in a preheated oven for a minute.

4. Remove the pie dishes from the oven. Pour batter into the pie dishes.

5. Drizzle the remaining oil over it and fold lightly.

6. Sprinkle remaining raisins, walnuts, pine nuts and rosemary.

7. Bake at 400°F for about 20-25 minutes until the top is cracked and brown.

8. Remove from oven and cool. Slice and serve either warm or cold with maple syrup.

French Apple Tart

Prep: 15 min	Total: 45 min	Servings: 12-15

Ingredients:

- 2 prebaked vegan pie crusts (9 inches each)

- 4 tablespoons sugar

- 8 Granny Smith apples, peeled, sliced into 1-inch-thick slices

- 2 teaspoons ground cinnamon

- 1/2 cup apricot jam mixed with about 2 tablespoons water

- 2 1/2 cups applesauce

Instructions:

1. Place a pan over medium heat. Add apple, sugar, and cinnamon to it. Stir and cook for about 3-4 minutes. Remove from heat and set aside till cool.

2. Spread apricot jam over the tart crusts. Next, spread applesauce over it.

3. Arrange the apple slices (slightly overlapping each other) all around the tart.

4. Place the tarts in a preheated oven at 400°F for about 20-30 minutes.

5. Slice into wedges when warm and serve topped with more apricot jam if desired.

French Toast Bread Pudding

Prep: 10 min	Total: 60 min	Servings: 8

Ingredients:

- 4 cups vegan French bread, cubed

- 1 tablespoon ground flaxseed

- 1 cup almond milk

- 2 medium bananas, thinly sliced

- 1 teaspoon ground cinnamon

- 1/2 tablespoon vanilla extract

- Maple syrup to taste

- Coconut cream to serve

Instructions:

1. Place bread cubes in a bowl.

2. Add almond milk, ground flax, cinnamon and vanilla to a bowl and whisk until well combined.

3. Pour this mixture over the bread and toss until bread is coated with the mixture.

4. Transfer this mixture into a greased baking dish.

5. Bake in a preheated oven for 40 minutes until browned on top. Slice when warm.

6. Drizzle maple syrup and serve with coconut cream.

Egyptian Apple Halawa

Prep: 15 min	Total: 60 min	Servings: 8

Ingredients:

- 10 apples, peeled, cored, roughly chopped into small pieces
- 10 tablespoons agave nectar or coconut palm sugar or to taste
- 4 tablespoons coconut oil
- 2 teaspoons ground cinnamon
- 20-25 pistachio nuts, unsalted, roughly chopped
- 4 teaspoons water

Instructions:

1. Place a skillet over medium high heat. Add oil. When oil melts, add apples and cook until brown.

2. Lower heat. Add water and cook until apples are tender, mashing simultaneously as it cooks.

3. Add agave nectar and cinnamon and cook until the mixture forms a lump.

4. Increase heat and stir until it becomes difficult to stir the mixture.

5. Line a baking dish with parchment paper. Transfer the mixture into it. Smoothen with the back of a spoon or spatula.

6. Sprinkle pistachio over it. Let it cool for a while. Chop into squares and serve when cooled.

Syrian Baklava

Prep: 10 min	Total: 60 min	Servings: 8

Ingredients:

For Baklava:

- 1/2 packet phyllo pastry sheets, thawed

- 3 tablespoons butter, melted

- 3 tablespoons hot water

- 1/4 cup ground almonds

- 25 grams' caster sugar

For filling:

- 1/2 cup +2 tablespoons pistachio nuts

- 1/2 tablespoon blossom water

- 1 tablespoon rosewater

- 1/2 tin fat-free condensed milk, sweetened

- 3 slices toasted bread, crust removed

  For syrup:

- 1/4 cup sugar

- 1/4 cup water

- 1/2 teaspoon lemon juice

- 1/2 tablespoon cornstarch

- 1/4 cup water to mix cornstarch

Instructions:

1. To make syrup: Add half-cup water to a
   saucepan. Place on medium heat. Add the sugar
   and bring to a boil, lower heat and simmer for 5-
   6 minutes.

2. Mix together in a small bowl the cornstarch and 1/4 cup water. Add this to the sugar solution. Stir constantly until thickened.

3. Remove from heat and lemon juice. Keep aside until cool.

4. For filling: Blend together all the ingredients of the filling and keep aside.

5. To make the baklava: In a small bowl, mix together almond powder and caster sugar

6. Grease an oven tray and place a phyllo pastry sheet on it. Brush with melted butter. Similarly, brush 2 more sheets with butter

7. Spread some filling all over one pastry sheet. Now, place 1 phyllo pastry sheet over the filling layer. Brush with butter.

8. Sprinkle some almond mixture over the 2nd sheet.

9. Repeat the process with the other 2 buttered phyllo sheets.

10. Brush the top surface with melted butter.

11. Bake in a preheated oven at 350°F until golden brown.

12. Remove from oven. Cut into diamond shape.

13. Pour the cooled syrup over it.

14. Cool and then serve.

Conclusion

I would like to thank you once again for downloading this book!

I want to reiterate that the Mediterranean Vegan diet is one of the most interesting combinations of two different types of dietary choices. In the course of this book you will learn to prepare different types of Mediterranean vegan meals without dairy products.

The recipes in this book are made using ingredients that are easily available in your local farmers' market. You can even play with the ingredients and choose ingredients that suit your taste buds. I would like to thank you once again for purchasing this book and sincerely hope that you found the book interesting and informative.

Made in the USA
Columbia, SC
27 February 2019